HANDS-ON HISTORY

PROJECTS ABOUT

Colonial Life

Marian Broida

BENCHMARK BOOKS

MARSHALL CAVENDISH
NEW YORK

Acknowledgments

Thanks to the following individuals and groups for their assistance: Martha B. Katz-Hyman, associate curator, and Marianne Martin, visual resources librarian, Colonial Williamsburg Foundation; Rachel and David Kleit; Carolyn Freeman Travers, research manager, Plimoth Plantation; and the staff at Jamestown Settlement and Yorktown Victory Center.

For helping test activities: Shaina Andres, Veronica Bauman, Zoe Baxter, Daniel Humphrey, Nicole Klionsky, Beatrice Misher, Nathan LaSala, and the View Ridge Boys' and Girls' Club.

The letter on page 34 is based on an actual letter by an eleven-year-old girl,
quoted on pages 159–160 of *Early Long Island: A Colonial Study*, Martha B. Flint, NY: G.P. Putnam's Sons, 1896.

Benchmark Books
Marshall Cavendish
99 White Plains Road
Tarrytown, NY 10591-9001
www.marshallcavendish.com

Library of Congress Cataloging-in-Publication Data

Broida, Marian.
  Projects about colonial life / by Marian Broida.
     v. cm. — (Hands-on history)
Includes bibliographical references and index.
Contents: Introduction — Northern colonies: Massachusetts — Middle
colonies: New York — Southern colonies: Virginia.
  ISBN 0-7614-1603-X
 1. United States—Social life and customs—To 1775—Study and
teaching—Activity programs—Juvenile literature. 2. United
States—History—Colonial period, ca. 1600-1775—Study and
teaching—Activity programs—Juvenile literature. [1. United
States—Social life and customs—Colonial period, ca. 1600-1775. 2.
United States—History—Colonial period, ca. 1600-1775. 3. Handicraft.]
I. Title. II. Series.
  E162.B865 2004
  973.2—dc21

                              2003001939

Illustrations and map by Rodica Prato

Copyright for all photographs belong to the photographer or agency
credited, unless specified otherwise.

Colonial Williamsburg Foundation: 40, 43. *Corbis:* Geoffrey Clements/Corbis, 1; Museum of the City of New York/Corbis, 4; Bettmann/Corbis, 15; North Carolina Museum of Art/Corbis, 18. *Hulton/Archive by Getty Images:* 8. *North Wind Picture Archives:* 6, 9, 26, 27, 28, 30, 36, 37.

Printed in China

3 5 6 4 2

Contents

⁓

This is how a nineteenth-century American artist imagined the landing of the Pilgrims at Plymouth.

1
Introduction

You are cooking breakfast over a fire in old New York. Your skin feels hot and your arms ache from stirring. Later you hear children reading aloud when you visit a one-room school with a very strict teacher.

In this book you will travel two hundred to four hundred years back in time. You will see for yourself how people once lived in the English colonies, before the United States became a nation.

On your trips to the past, you will meet young Benjamin Franklin, Pilgrims, African American slaves, and other colonists in Massachusetts, New York, and Virginia. During your visits you will mold candles, make a model windmill, write with a **quill** pen, and bake cookies called Shrewsbury cakes.

We hope you enjoy your journey to the past.

This engraving shows the city of Boston, Massachusetts, in the 1660s.

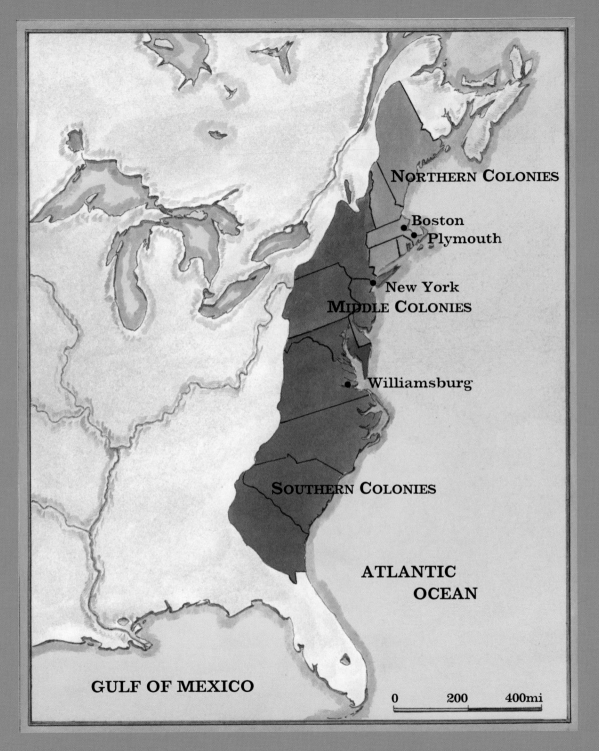

NORTHERN COLONIES

Boston
Plymouth

New York
MIDDLE COLONIES

Williamsburg

SOUTHERN COLONIES

ATLANTIC
OCEAN

GULF OF MEXICO

0   200   400mi

This map shows the thirteen English colonies that declared independence from England in 1776. They are divided into three groups. Northern colonies are in blue, middle colonies are in purple, and southern colonies are in red. Black dots show some of the places you will visit in this book. What is now the state of Maine was originally part of the Massachusetts colony.

The busy port of Salem, Massachusetts, around 1780.

2

The Northern Colonies

In 1620 the Pilgrims started the first northern **colony** when their ship *Mayflower* landed at a spot called Plymouth. Pilgrims belonged to a religious group known as Puritans. They had left England seeking religious freedom for themselves. The Puritans farmed the rocky soil and built many small towns. The city of Boston, Massachusetts, began as a Puritan town.

In time the northern colonies grew to include Massachusetts, New Hampshire, Rhode Island, and Connecticut. This area became known as New England, as most of the settlers came from England.

Cod fishermen off the coast of New England.

Fishnet

It is 1622, a calm spring day in Plymouth. The bluefish and bass are thick in the harbor waters. Your father is heading out to go fishing with his mates.

You hand him a new fishnet, the first one you have made yourself.

"That's good work," he says, running the knotted twine through his fingers. "You're good with your hands." He smiles. "I hope we bring your net back full of fish."

You will need:

- 9 yards jute, hemp twine, or cotton string
- rough stick with bark, 12 to 16 inches long
- scissors
- chair

1. Tie a piece of cord to the stick in two places, one at each end of the stick. The cord should be long enough to hang over the back of a chair.

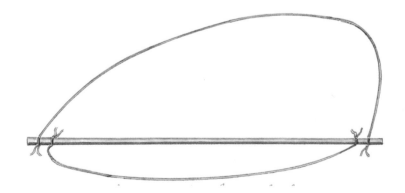

2. Cut another piece of cord an inch longer than the stick. This will be the "main cord." Tie the main cord to the stick at each end (see illustration). Hang the longer cord over the chair, as shown.

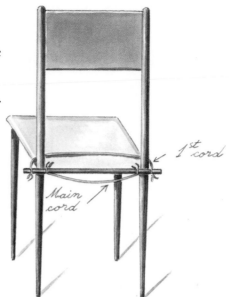

3. Cut five pieces of cord, each about 4 feet long. Fold one piece in half.

4. Lay the folded end over the main cord, pointing away from you.

5. Pull the fold slightly below the main cord, as shown.

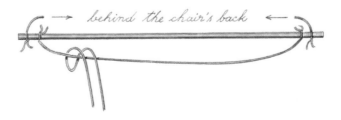

behind the chair's back

6. Poke the two tails of the folded cord through the fold,
away from you. Pull tightly.

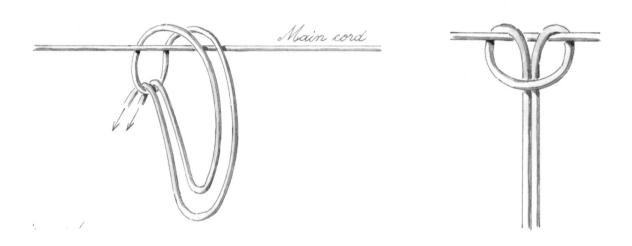

7. Repeat with the other four cords. Space them evenly along the main cord.
You now have five pairs of cords hanging down.

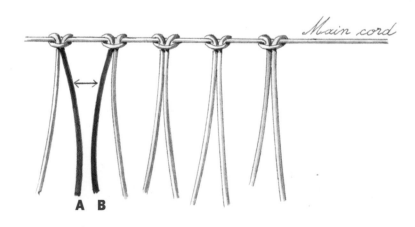

8. Take the RIGHT cord from the left-most pair (A). Tie it to its neighbor, which is the LEFT cord from the pair next to it (B). Hold the two cords side by side. Shape them into a loop, with the two tails crossing over the hanging ones from right to left. Pull the tails of both cords through the loop, back to front. Before pulling them tightly, make sure the knot is where you want it, 1 to 2 inches below the main cord.

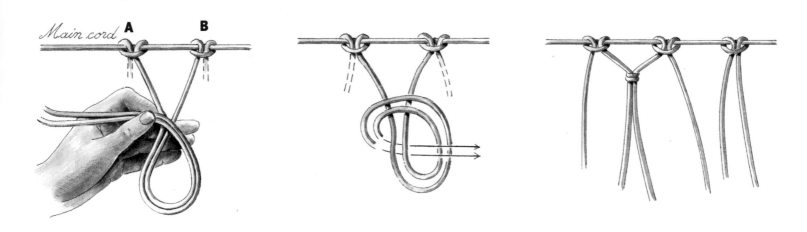

9. Let go of the cords you have just been working with. Find the next two neighbors to the right. Tie them together the same way. Place this knot so it is at the same height as the first. Repeat until you have four knots in a row. There will be a loose, unknotted cord all the way on the left and all the way on the right.

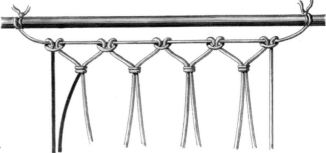

10. Now drop down 1 to 2 inches. Find the free cord on the left and tie it to its neighbor, as you did before. Repeat step 9 all the way across.

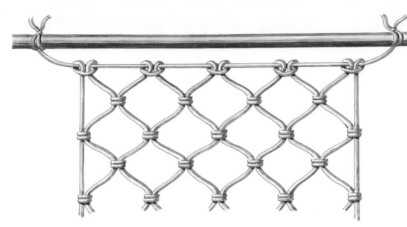

11. Keep making rows of knots until you run out of cord. Finish each row across before dropping to the next.

12. Remove the main cord from the stick.

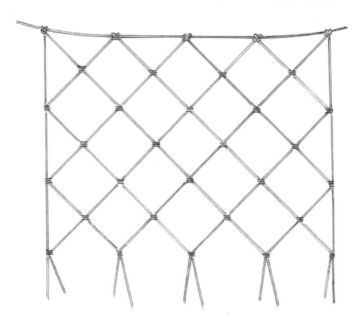

Hornbook

It is 1675. You are in a one-room school-house in a small town. The teacher hands your little brother a **hornbook**—a flat piece of wood with a handle. Tacked onto it is a printed page. The page is covered with a piece of animal horn that is thin enough to see through.

"Read the alphabet, please," the teacher says.

Your brother reads several letters, then stops. "I don't know this letter," he whispers.

"Then you'll wear a dunce cap all day!" says the teacher.

Hornbooks usually showed the alphabet, a few syllables, and a prayer.

You will need:

- strong scissors
- corrugated cardboard, about 8½ by 5½ inches
- paper
- pen
- ruler
- colored tape or masking tape, ½- or ¾- inch wide
- piece of clear, heavy plastic about 4½ by 5 inches from report cover or plastic photo pocket, for example
- white glue

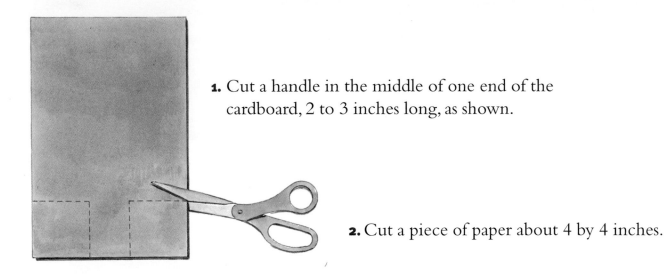

1. Cut a handle in the middle of one end of the cardboard, 2 to 3 inches long, as shown.

2. Cut a piece of paper about 4 by 4 inches.

3. Draw a border about a thumbnail's width inside the edges of the paper. A ruler will help keep your lines straight.

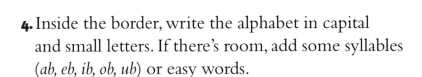

4. Inside the border, write the alphabet in capital and small letters. If there's room, add some syllables (*ab, eb, ib, ob, ub*) or easy words.

5. Trace around the paper onto the plastic. Cut out the plastic.

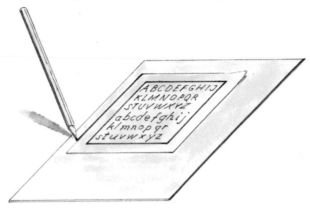

6. Glue the paper to the cardboard.

7. Cover the paper with the plastic.

8. Attach the plastic to the cardboard by fastening colored tape neatly around all four edges of the plastic. Cut the tape instead of tearing it so the ends are square.

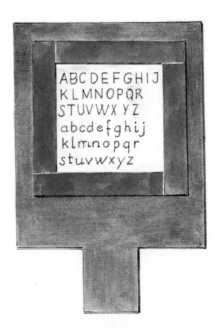

At age twelve, Benjamin Franklin became his brother's apprentice and learned to print books. Later he became a publisher, author, inventor, scientist, postmaster, and signer of the Declaration of Independence and the Constitution.

Candle Making

The year is 1717. You are in Boston, Massachusetts, playing with your friend Benjamin Franklin. "What kind of work does your father do?" you ask.

"He's a **chandler**," says Ben. "He makes candles from **tallow**—melted animal fat. Sometimes I help him cut wicks for the candles and pour tallow into the molds. When the molds cool, he takes out the candles."

"Will you be a chandler someday?"

"My father wants me to," says Ben, "but I have a dislike for the trade. Tallow smells terrible."

You will need:

- small foam paintbrush
- 1 teaspoon cooking oil
- clean, dry tin can without lid, 28 ounces or larger
- newspaper
- 1/2 pound paraffin*
- old table knife
- hammer
- crayon with the paper peeled off
- large pot
- stove

- water
- old spoon or stick for stirring
- scissors
- about 3 feet cotton twine or candlewicks
- 2 or more paper clips
- 2 or more pencils
- pot holder
- 2 or more disposable cups for molds, 6- to 10-ounce size; waxed paper, Styrofoam, or flexible plastic
- refrigerator

*available in craft stores

1. Important: have an adult help the whole time.

2. With the paintbrush, spread the oil lightly all over the inside of the can.

3. Spread out the newspaper, and put the paraffin on top. Use the knife and hammer to hack off enough chunks to half fill the can. Add a crayon.

4. Put the pot on the stove. Don't light it yet. Pour about 2 inches of water into the pot. Place the can in the water. If the can floats, take it out and pour a little water out of the pot. Be sure not to get water in the can.

5. Turn the stove on at low heat.

6. Stir the wax now and then.

7. Meanwhile, cut a piece of string or wick about 4 inches longer than the height of your molds. Tie one end of the string to a paper clip. Tie the other end around a pencil and lay the pencil across the top of a mold. Roll the string around the pencil until the string hangs straight, with the clip flat on the bottom of the mold. Repeat with the rest of your molds.

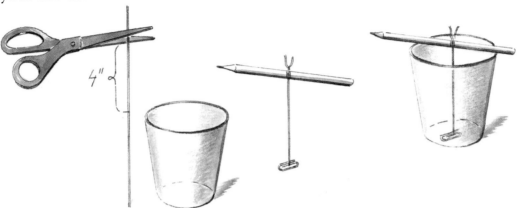

8. Have an adult remove the can with a pot holder as soon as the last of the wax is melted.

9. Set the molds on newspaper. Have an adult pour melted wax into each one.

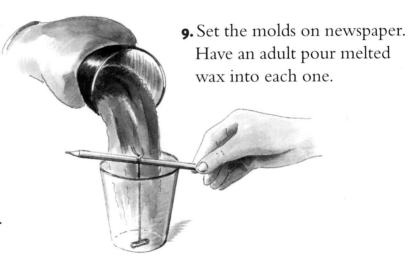

10. Refrigerate the molds overnight.

11. Cut or peel each cup away from the candle. Trim the wicks to about ½ inch.

Building a Cradle

It is 1750. You are eating a midday meal with your family and John, your father's **apprentice**. Your father is a **joiner**, or woodworker. He is teaching fifteen-year-old John to build furniture. In exchange, John will work for your father until he is twenty-one.

"Mr. Colman has asked us to build him a cradle, John," says your father. "His wife will have a baby come spring. Think you can make a cradle by yourself?"

"I can try, sir," says John, looking proud. You smile at him across the table.

You will need:

- pen
- lidless box about 6 inches long, 3 to 4 inches wide, and 1 inch deep, such as a box that checks come in
- poster board or cereal-box cardboard, about 8 by 8 inches square
- scissors
- circle of corrugated cardboard, 6 to 7 inches across
- duct tape
- newspaper
- paintbrushes
- acrylic paints
- rags and fabric scraps, optional

1. Trace around the box bottom onto the poster board (or thin cardboard) twice. Cut out the two rectangles. Fold each in half, making shapes like squares. Unfold one and cut it along the crease.

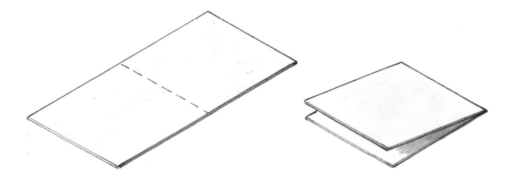

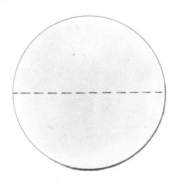

2. Cut the thick cardboard circle in half. Tape one half to each end of the box, as shown. The flat part of the half circle lines up with the top edge of the box. The round part hangs below. (See illustration on next page.)

3. Unfold the biggest piece of poster board halfway, making an L shape. Tape the L upside down to one end of the box, as shown. It will form a hood for the cradle. Leave some space between the top of the hood and the box.

4. Tape the other two pieces of poster board to the box, making the sides of the hood.

5. Use more duct tape as needed to strengthen the cradle.

6. Spread out newspaper to protect your work surface, and paint the cradle.

7. If you like, make a mattress and bedding from fabric you can find. Colonial babies often slept on cloth sacks filled with straw or rags.

Colonial children were given many rules. Here are a few from *The School of Manners*, a book published in England in 1701 and used throughout the American colonies:

Feed thy self with thy two Fingers, and the Thumb of the left hand.

Stuff not thy mouth so as to fill thy Cheeks. Be content with smaller Mouthfulls.

Spit not in the Room, but in a corner, and rub it out with thy Foot.

3

The Middle Colonies: New York

New York, New Jersey, Pennsylvania, and Delaware made up the middle colonies. Settlers moved there from the Netherlands, Sweden, Germany, and England.

In 1664, England took over the Dutch colony of New Netherland, renaming part of it New York. Most of the Dutch settlers stayed. Their town New Amsterdam, part of New Netherland, was also renamed New York. By the mid-1700s it had become one of the largest cities in the English colonies.

Taverns, like this one in New Amsterdam, were favorite gathering places.

Cooking Sappawn

The year is 1670. It is early morning in New York town. You are stirring a pot hanging on a hook over the fire. The fireplace is decorated with blue-and-white tiles from the Netherlands. Inside the pot, cornmeal mush is bubbling slowly.

Your baby brother tugs at your clothes. You carry him to your mother, away from the flames.

"Careful the sappawn doesn't stick!" she says.

You rush back to the fire. Everyone will be annoyed if you burn breakfast!

Today we can make a meal in a few minutes, but in the days before microwaves and packaged foods, meals often took hours to prepare. One of the quickest colonial dishes was cornmeal mush, called sappawn in New Netherland and hasty pudding in the British colonies. It needed frequent stirring over a fire for about thirty minutes. That probably does not seem so "hasty" to you!

You will need:

- measuring cups and spoons
- 4 cups milk
- ¼ cup cornmeal
- 1 teaspoon salt
- large pot
- wooden spoon
- timer
- pot holder or hot pad
- raisins, sugar, or maple syrup, optional

This recipe serves four people.

1. Ask an adult for help.

2. Measure the milk, cornmeal, and salt into the pot.

3. Cook the mixture on low heat, stirring often.

4. When steam starts rising, set the timer for twelve to thirty minutes. (The longer it cooks, the better it tastes.) Now stir without stopping until the timer rings. Colonial food takes patience!

5. Remove the pot from the heat. Turn off the stove. Set the pot on a pot holder to cool a bit. Spoon the warm sappawn into bowls. If you like, add sweetening, raisins, or more milk.

Model Windmill

It is 1675. On your way home from your uncle's house, you pass a windmill on a hill. You stop to watch the wind turn its four blades. You know that inside wheat is being ground into flour between two flat, heavy stones. The wind provides the power to move the upper stone, mashing the grain beneath.

From a window the miller sees you watching. "What, don't you have any work to do?" he calls.

"Good day, sir!" you call back. "I'm on my way to do it!"

English as well as Dutch colonists used windmills to grind grain and saw logs.

You will need:

- clean, empty milk carton, 1-quart size
- handful of small rocks or dried beans
- 2 strips of poster board, each 1 by 10 inches
- ruler
- pen
- scissors
- Scotch tape
- 8 by 2 inch piece of felt
- small piece of aluminum foil
- 1½-inch long nail
- cork (from craft store or wine bottle)
- electric fan
- duct tape

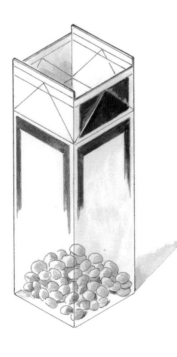

1. Ask an adult for help.

2. Open the top of the carton fully. Put in the rocks.

3. Lay the ruler beside each poster board strip, as shown. Make dots at 3 inches and 7 inches on each strip.

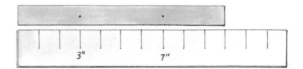

4. Carefully cut a ½-inch slit halfway across the poster board at the 3-inch dot. Do the same at the 7-inch dot, but start the slit on the other side of the strip. Repeat on the other strip.

5. Make a plus sign with the two strips, forming four wings. Important: make sure the slit is on the same side of all four wings as shown. (You may have to turn one strip over.) Scotch tape the two strips together in the middle.

6. Fold up the right edge of each wing from the slit to the end of the strip, as shown.

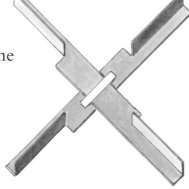

7. Cut fourteen pieces of felt, all the size of postage stamps. Cut one piece of foil the same size.

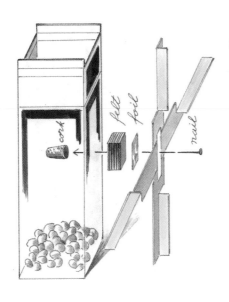

8. Poke the nail through the middle of the plus, through the foil square, and through all the felt squares. Poke it through the milk carton, just beneath the folded part. Carefully push the cork onto the nail's tip, inside the carton.

9. Place your windmill right in front of the fan. Does it turn? If it does, tape the top closed with duct tape. If not, check to see if the windmill blades are touching the carton. If they are, add more felt.

33

Writing with a **Quill Pen**

The year is 1770. Your mother has asked you to write a letter to your grandfather. On your first two tries, your pen leaves a great big blot of ink on the page. So far your third try is coming out well. You read your words proudly:

Ever Honored Grandfather:
Sir: I want to tell you that I have already
made a Confiderable Progrefs in Learning.
I have already gone through fome Rules of
Arithmetic. In a little Time I fhall be able
to give a Better account of my Learning.

Your moft obedient Grandchild,

Colonists wrote a small *s* two ways. At the end of a word it looks like our lowercase *s*. At the beginning or middle of a word, it resembles our small *f*.

1. Gently place the tip of the feather in the water. Soak it a few minutes to soften the shaft.

2. Cut the tip at an angle, as shown.

3. Make a small straight slit (about ¼-inch) leading straight up the shaft from the point.

4. Dip the tip in the ink.

5. Try writing a letter. When the pen runs dry, dip it back in the ink. Watch out for blots!

Slaves greeting the plantation owner's family in Virginia around 1700.

The Southern Colonies: Virginia

In 1607, English people built their first permanent colony in America at Jamestown, Virginia. In time, England set up five southern colonies: Maryland, Virginia, North Carolina, South Carolina, and Georgia.

Many southern colonists owned small farms. The wealthiest owned huge farms called **plantations**. The poorest people, the slaves, owned nothing. The law said their masters owned them.

Slaves lived in all the colonies. In the South they did farmwork and housework and practiced skilled trades such as laying bricks.

The kitchen at Monticello, Thomas Jefferson's Virginia home. Southern kitchens were often separate from the main building, which helped prevent house fires and kept the main house cooler.

Baking Shrewsbury Cakes

It is 1760. You are sweeping the kitchen building where your mother, a slave, works as a cook. She has just taken a pan of Shrewsbury cakes from the oven.

She sees you eyeing them. "You want one? Watch out," she says. "Mistress will whip you if she catches you."

Through the window you can see the main house. No one is coming toward the kitchen. "I'm not afraid," you say. Just in case, you cram the whole cookie into your mouth at once.

You will need:

- oven
- large bowl
- 2 cookie sheets
- large spoon
- measuring cups and spoons
- electric mixer or lots of time
- teaspoon
- pot holder
- spatula
- 1 stick (½ cup) of butter at room temperature
- ½ cup sugar
- 1 egg
- ½ cup flour
- ½ teaspoon nutmeg
- plate or wire rack

1. Get adult permission or help. Preheat the oven to 350 degrees Fahrenheit.

2. Rub the cookie sheets with a small amount of butter.

3. Put the rest of the butter into the bowl. Break it up a little with the spoon. Add the sugar. Mix with the mixer or beat by hand for several minutes.

4. Stir in the egg. Mix again.

5. Stir in the flour and nutmeg. Mix until batter becomes smooth.

6. Place teaspoons of batter onto the cookie sheets, 2 inches apart. Bake about ten minutes or until the edges turn brown.

7. Remove from the oven with pot holders. Use the spatula and a pot holder to take the cookies off the sheets and place them on a plate or rack to cool.

Sewing a Pocket

It is 1765. Sarah is searching for her pocket—the flat pouch she ties around her waist under her skirt.

"Rachel, have you seen my pocket?" she asks. She looks sharply at her sister's face. "Did you borrow it again?"

Her sister blushes.

"You'd better stop taking it," says Sarah, "or I'll sew it to my skirt."

"Silly!" says Rachel. "Everyone will laugh at you if you do!"

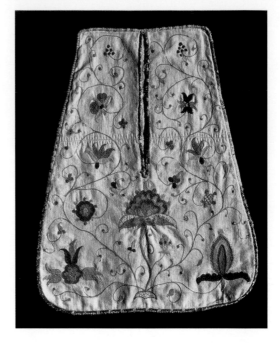

In colonial times women's skirts had no pockets. Instead, girls and women wore separate pockets on cords around their waists. They reached into them through slits in the sides of their skirts.

You will need:

- piece of light-colored felt, about 9 by 12 inches
- 4 safety pins
- ballpoint pen
- sharp scissors
- needle
- thread
- 4 feet of ribbon at least ½-inch wide—cloth ribbon is best
- colored permanent markers

1. Fold the felt in half, so it's about 9 by 6 inches. Pin it together in four spots as shown.

2. Using almost the whole piece of felt, draw a pocket shape with the pen, as shown. Cut through both pieces of felt, following the shape you have just drawn. Take out the pins. You will now have two pocket shapes.

3. On one piece, draw a line down the middle. Start about 1 inch from the top, and end at least 1 inch from the bottom.

4. Make a cut where the line is on that piece only. Hint: to start, pinch up a fold as shown and cut through it along the line.

5. Pin the two pocket shapes back together so the edges match.

6. Thread the needle. Tie the thread ends together in a knot. Stitch the felt pieces together around the sides and bottom. Use a stitch that wraps around the side, so you always push the needle down through the felt, never up.

7. When 4 to 5 inches of thread remain free, have an adult help you knot the ends. **DO NOT** wait until your thread is shorter than this. Cut off the extra thread and needle.

8. Thread your needle with a new piece and continue sewing.

9. When you have stitched all but the top, knot the end of the thread, cut off the extra thread, and remove the pins.

10. Decorate the side with the slit with markers. That side will go in front.

11. Pin the ribbon to the outside of the pocket. Tie the ribbon around your waist with the pocket over your hip. Keep a handkerchief or tissue inside.

Money: Pieces of Eight

It is 1774. You are playing outside your house in Williamsburg when you see something shiny on the ground. It is a bit of silver, shaped like a pie slice.

"Is that money?" your sister asks.

"Yes," you say. "It's part of a silver dollar from Spain. Someone cut the coin in half, and in half again, and in half again. Eight of these would make a dollar."

"Can we keep it?" asks your sister.

"We'd best ask Mother," you say, thinking of all the sweets you could buy.

In the British colonies, people used money minted in England, Spain, and America. People sometimes cut Spanish dollars into pieces to make change. Spanish silver dollars are called pieces of eight.

You will need:

- oven
- empty vitamin jar with cap
- ¼ block of Sculpey*
- aluminum foil
- scissors

- blunt knife (plastic is fine)
- ballpoint pen or toothpick
- white glue
- cookie sheet

*available at craft stores

1. Get adult permission or help. Preheat the oven according to the directions on the Sculpey package.

2. Place the Sculpey on a piece of foil, and use the jar to roll it out until it is about as thick as a quarter.

3. Use the jar lid as a cookie cutter. Make up to three clay circles.

4. For each circle, cut out two aluminum-foil squares with the scissors, slightly larger than the clay circles.

44

5. With the knife or your hands, move each clay circle onto its own foil square.

6. Lay another foil square on top of each clay circle and press down firmly, making a clay "sandwich." Cut off the extra foil around each circle. Wrap up the edges to make a foil-covered coin.

7. Using the pen or toothpick, copy the picture from one of the coins shown on page 43 on one or both sides. Or you can design your own patterns. Be careful not to break through the foil.

8. Press the coin with the bottom of the jar. The picture should still be there.

9. Cut the coins into halves, quarters, or eighths, shaped like slices of pie.

10. Put the slices on a fresh piece of foil. Place the foil on a cookie sheet and bake for six to eight minutes. Remove from oven and let the slices cool. If the foil falls off, glue it back on.

11. Store your pieces of eight in a pocket or small bag.

Glossary

apprentice: Someone learning a trade by working under a master. Most colonial apprentices were teenagers.

chandler: A person who makes candles for a living.

colony: A group of people who leave their own country and settle in another distant land but who keep close ties to their home country; the land settled by this group of people.

hornbook: A wooden paddle holding a printed page covered with a thin sheet of animal horn, used to help children learn to read.

joiner: Someone who joins pieces of wood to build furniture and the insides of houses.

pieces of eight: Spanish silver dollars, sometimes cut into pieces.

plantations: Large estates or farms worked by laborers who live there. Until the end of the Civil War, plantations were worked by slaves as well as by freemen, white and black.

quill: The shaft of a feather, or a pen made from one.

tallow: Animal fat, usually from cows.

Metric Conversion Chart

You can use the chart below to convert from U. S. measurements to the metric system.

Weight
1 ounce = 28 grams
½ pound (8 ounces) = 227 grams
1 pound = .45 kilogram
2.2 pounds = 1 kilogram

Liquid volume
1 teaspoon = 5 milliliters
1 tablespoon = 15 milliliters
1 fluid ounce = 30 milliliters
1 cup = 240 milliliters (.24 liter)
1 pint = 480 milliliters (.48 liter)
1 quart = .95 liter

Length
¼ inch = .6 centimeter
½ inch = 1.25 centimeters
1 inch = 2.5 centimeters

Temperature
100°F = 40°C
110°F = 45°C
350°F = 180°C
375°F = 190°C
400°F = 200°C
425°F = 220°C
450°F = 235°C

Find Out More

Web Sites:

Colonial Williamsburg, Virginia
www.colonialwilliamsburg.org/

Monticello, Virginia (Thomas Jefferson's home)
www.monticello.org/index.html

Mount Vernon, Virginia (George Washington's home)
www.mountvernon.org/

Philipsburg Manor, Historic Hudson Valley, New York
www.hudsonvalley.org/web/phil-main.html

Plimoth Plantation, Plymouth, Massachusetts
www.plimoth.org/

Books

Anderson, Joan. *A Williamsburg Household*. New York: Clarion Books, 1988.

Barrett, Tracy. *Growing Up in Colonial America*. Brookfield, CT: Millbrook Press, 1995.

Bowen, Gary. *Stranded at Plimoth Plantation, 1626*. New York: HarperCollins, 1994.

Haskins, James and Kathleen Benson. *Building a New Land: African Americans in Colonial America*. New York: HarperCollins, 2001.

Kent, Deborah. *In the Southern Colonies*. New York: Marshall Cavendish, 2000.

McGovern, Ann. *If You Lived in Colonial Times*. New York: Scholastic Inc., 1964, 1992.

About the Author

Marian Broida has a special interest in hands-on history for children. Growing up near George Washington's home in Mount Vernon, Virginia, Ms. Broida spent much of her childhood pretending she lived in colonial America. In addition to children's activity books, she writes books for adults on health care topics and occasionally works as a nurse. Ms. Broida lives in Seattle, Washington.

Index

Page numbers in **boldface** are illustrations.